AND SO THE TORCH IS PASSED TO THE NEXT GENERATION OF STARS...

The greatest football players win championships.

They set records.

They burn their accomplishments into our collective memory.

And when they are gone, we miss them.

We wonder how they can ever be replaced. Those stars from the past with names like Elway and Marino, Lott and Payton, Alworth and Aikman. But that's the beauty of professional football. There is always someone new waiting in the wings. Youth succeeds age. There is always a new crop of rising stars ready to take the field, to make the plays, to win championships.

The game is in good hands.

Dwight
FREENEY

RISING STARS

NFL

by **JOE LAYDEN**

SCHOLASTIC INC.

New York   Toronto   London   Auckland   Sydney
Mexico City   New Delhi   Hong Kong   Buenos Aires

ISBN 0-439-80247-4

12 11 10 9 8 7 6 5 4 3 2 1   5 6 7 8 9 10/0

Printed in the U.S.A.
First printing, August 2005
Book design by Michael Malone

> "I'm a **blue-collar** player: a guy who **works hard, doesn't complain** too much, and makes plays."

DEFENSIVE END
INDIANAPOLIS COLTS

BORN: 1/4/78
HEIGHT: 6-1
WEIGHT: 268
COLLEGE: SYRACUSE

SACK KING

Everyone knows all about the Indianapolis Colts and their high-powered offense, led by quarterback Peyton Manning. But you don't win games without defense, and as the Colts rolled to another divisional title, no one was more pivotal than Dwight Freeney. Imagine how it must feel to line up against Dwight. He's a little on the small side for a defensive end, but he's strong and smart. Most important of all, he has one of the quickest first steps in the NFL. If you blink or make a mistake—forget it!—Dwight is gone. The next thing you know, he's in the backfield, blanketing the quarterback for another of his famous sacks. Dwight likes to think of himself as a quiet, steady player. But sacks are high profile, and Dwight gets a lot of them. In fact, he led the NFL with a club-record 16 sacks in 2004 and was named All-Pro. But you won't hear much about this from Dwight. He likes to let his game do the talking.

DID YOU KNOW?

DWIGHT IS ONE OF THE NFL'S OUTSTANDING ALL-AROUND ATHLETES. IN HIGH SCHOOL HE PLAYED FOUR VARSITY SPORTS: FOOTBALL, BASKETBALL, BASEBALL, AND SOCCER.

FREENEY BY THE NUMBERS
2004 SEASON

TOTAL TACKLES: 34 • SOLO TACKLES: 31 • ASSISTS: 3
SACKS: 16 • FORCED FUMBLES: 4

ANTONIO GATES

"A **dunk** is nice because it can **create momentum,** but it's not as good as **scoring** a **touchdown."**

TIGHT END
SAN DIEGO CHARGERS

BORN: 6/18/80
HEIGHT: 6-4
WEIGHT: 260
COLLEGE: KENT STATE

THE NATURAL

It happens all the time. Antonio Gates leaps high over a defender to haul in a spectacular reception, prompting someone to suggest that he might want to test his athleticism on a basketball court. Sorry. Been there, done that. You see, back when he was a high school senior in Detroit, Antonio had to make a decision. He was an all-state selection in both basketball and football, but it just wasn't possible to play both sports in college. So Antonio chose basketball, his first love. At Kent State he was the best player on the team and an honorable mention All-America. But he never stopped thinking about football. In 2003 Antonio joined the Chargers as a free agent. He was a little rusty at first, but before long he began shredding opposing defenses. Within a year, he was the most celebrated tight end in the NFL. Antonio still plays pickup basketball once in a while, but now everything has changed. Football isn't just his game. It's his life.

DID YOU KNOW?

ANTONIO HOLDS THE NFL SINGLE-SEASON RECORD WITH 13 TOUCHDOWN RECEPTIONS BY A TIGHT END.

GATES BY THE NUMBERS
2004 SEASON

RECEPTIONS: 81 • RECEIVING YARDS: 964 • YARDS PER CATCH: 11.9
LONGEST RECEPTION: 72 • TOUCHDOWNS: 13

Andre JOHNSON

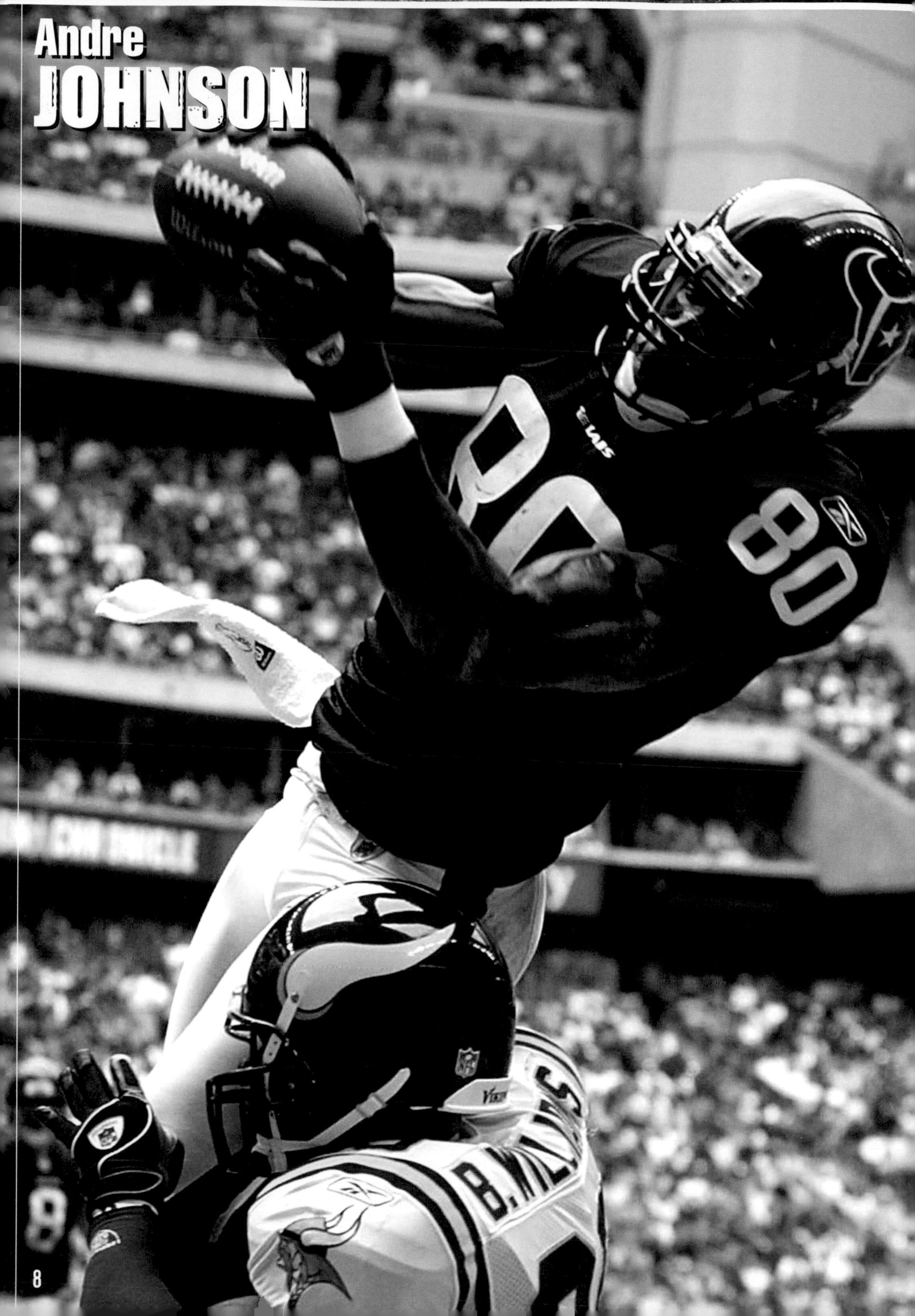

> **"I try to be consistent every time** I'm out on the field, whether it's a **game or practice."**

**WIDE RECEIVER
HOUSTON TEXANS**

BORN: 7/11/81
HEIGHT: 6-3
WEIGHT: 219
COLLEGE: MIAMI

QUIET CONFIDENCE

In just two seasons, Andre Johnson has become one of the best receivers in the NFL. With a dynamic combination of size and speed (he was a champion sprinter in college), Andre makes fans hold their breath in anticipation every time the ball is snapped. He makes the impossible seem routine. In a game against the Kansas City Chiefs, for example, Andre leaped over a defender, tipped the ball into the air, and juggled it several times before catching it as he crashed to the ground. In another game he caught 12 passes for 170 yards and two touchdowns, including several that required the skill of an acrobat. It was the kind of performance that left his teammates awestruck. "I've never seen anyone play football like that," says Texans tight end Billy Miller. "Andre is as good as anyone in the NFL." The praise is left to others, for Andre is as quiet off the field as he is explosive on it. And that's saying a lot.

DID YOU KNOW?

ANDRE HAS SOMETHING OF A NEED FOR SPEED. HIS AMBITION IS TO ONE DAY TAKE A RIDE IN A FIGHTER JET.

**JOHNSON BY THE NUMBERS
2004 SEASON** ▶ RECEPTIONS: 79 • RECEIVING YARDS: 1,142 • YARDS PER CATCH: 14.5
LONGEST RECEPTION: 54 • TOUCHDOWNS: 6

Julius
JONES

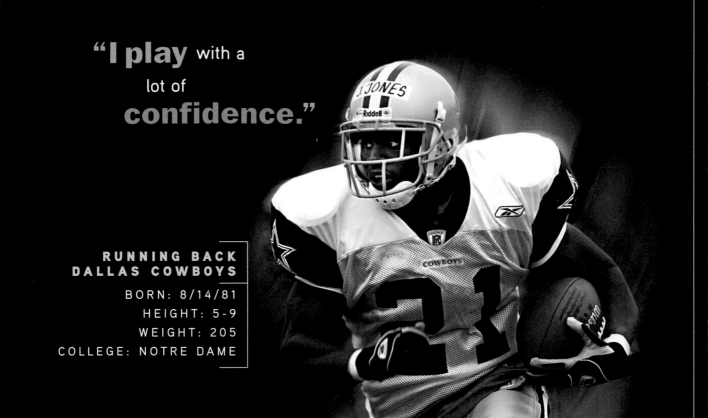

"**I play** with a lot of **confidence.**"

**RUNNING BACK
DALLAS COWBOYS**

BORN: 8/14/81
HEIGHT: 5-9
WEIGHT: 205
COLLEGE: NOTRE DAME

LITTLE BIG MAN

Maybe Julius Jones feels likes he has something to prove. After all, 43 players were taken ahead of him in the 2004 NFL Draft. Not until midway through the second round did the Dallas Cowboys finally choose the explosive little running back from the University of Notre Dame. But you can be sure of one thing: a lot of teams now realize they made a mistake. Julius Jones can flat-out play. "Certain players in professional sports just have it," says Julius' teammate, Keyshawn Johnson. "And Julius has it." Despite missing half of his rookie season with a broken shoulder blade, Julius led the Cowboys in rushing and proved to be a star in the making. He's short and compact, with a sprinter's speed and a gymnast's sense of balance — just try to knock him off his feet! And then get out of the way, because Julius will still be running!

DID YOU KNOW?

FOOTBALL RUNS IN THE JONES FAMILY. JULIUS' BIG BROTHER, THOMAS, WAS AN ALL-AMERICA AT VIRGINIA AND A FIRST-ROUND DRAFT PICK IN 2000.

**JONES BY THE NUMBERS
2004 SEASON** ▶ RUSHING YARDS: 819 • YARDS PER CARRY: 4.2 • TOUCHDOWNS: 7
RECEPTIONS: 17 • RECEIVING YARDS: 109

Byron
LEFTWICH

> "I never looked at myself as a **rookie.** I was the **quarterback** and the **leader** of the team."

QUARTERBACK
JACKSONVILLE JAGUARS

BORN: 1/14/80
HEIGHT: 6-5
WEIGHT: 245
COLLEGE: MARSHALL

NO FEAR

Let's turn back the clock to September of 2003. First-round draft pick Byron Leftwich is standing on the sidelines, dutifully charting stats for the Jacksonville Jaguars. Suddenly the action stops. The Jags' starting quarterback is hurt. Byron drops his clipboard, straps on his helmet, and jogs onto the field. You don't get to choose when you play in the NFL. Opportunity knocks—sometimes at the expense of others—and you simply answer the door. Ever since that day, Byron Leftwich has been a starter, and one of the NFL's most exciting young players. With an arm that never seems to tire and the poise of a seasoned veteran, he's ready to join the ranks of the game's most prolific passers. His 2,819 yards passing in 2003 was the fourth-highest total ever for a rookie. And he was even better in 2004. Byron is one of the NFL's new breed of quarterbacks: big, strong, and supremely confident. Challenge him at your own risk.

DID YOU KNOW? BYRON IS THE SECOND CONSECUTIVE QUARTERBACK FROM MARSHALL TO MAKE A BIG SPLASH IN THE NFL. THE FIRST WAS CHAD PENNINGTON OF THE NEW YORK JETS.

LEFTWICH BY THE NUMBERS
2004 SEASON ▶ COMPLETIONS: 267 • ATTEMPTS: 441 • PASSING YARDS: 2,941
TOUCHDOWNS: 15 • RATING: 82.2

Eli
MANNING

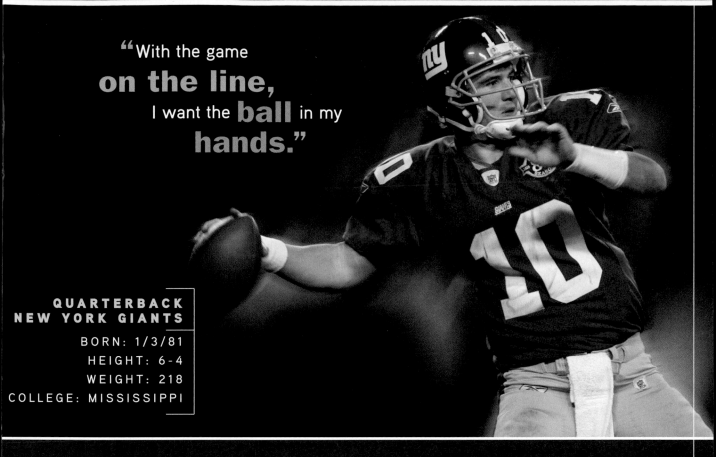

QUARTERBACK
NEW YORK GIANTS

BORN: 1/3/81
HEIGHT: 6-4
WEIGHT: 218
COLLEGE: MISSISSIPPI

GREAT EXPECTATIONS

The official "arrival" of Eli Manning came late in the season, in a game against the powerful Pittsburgh Steelers. There he was, standing in the pocket, calmly firing one bull's-eye after another, as the Giants nearly pulled off one of the biggest upsets of the year. It was the kind of performance everyone had expected of Eli, and now, after several long afternoons, he had delivered. There was no turning back. It wasn't an easy rookie season for Eli. After all, when you grow up in football's First Family, people expect a lot. Eli's dad, Archie Manning, was an NFL star in the 1970s. His big brother is Colts quarterback Peyton Manning, who has been rewriting the record books almost since he arrived in the NFL. Now it's Eli's turn. The Giants made him a starter midway through the 2004 season, and he showed flashes of brilliance. Eli is a natural leader with a great arm and a fearless approach to the game. Guess it runs in the family.

DID YOU KNOW?

ELI HAS ANOTHER OLDER BROTHER, COOPER, WHO ALSO PLAYED FOOTBALL AT THE UNIVERSITY OF MISSISSIPPI, BUT COOPER'S CAREER WAS CUT SHORT BY A NECK INJURY.

MANNING BY THE NUMBERS
2004 SEASON

COMPLETIONS: 95 • ATTEMPTS: 197 • PASSING YARDS: 1,043
TOUCHDOWNS: 6 • RATING: 55.4

Willis
McGAHEE

"Never **look back—bad things** might happen.**"**

RUNNING BACK
BUFFALO BILLS

BORN: 10/20/81
HEIGHT: 6-0
WEIGHT: 228
COLLEGE: MIAMI

COMEBACK KID

When you watch him play now, you'd never guess that Willis McGahee's career nearly ended before it began. He slithers through the narrowest of openings and bursts into the secondary with incredible speed. Once in the open field, Willis is nearly impossible to track down. It's hard to believe that his left knee was reconstructed. That's right—Willis suffered a devastating injury while playing for the University of Miami. Some people wondered whether he'd ever be able to make it in the NFL. But not Willis. He worked hard to recover from surgery. The Bills admired his attitude and courage. They made Willis a first-round draft pick, and he didn't disappoint them. Today, Willis is one of the league's most versatile young running backs and a fan favorite in Buffalo. That's no surprise. After all, everyone likes a story with a happy ending.

DID YOU KNOW?

WILLIS WAS ONE OF THE MOST EXCITING OFFENSIVE PLAYERS IN UNIVERSITY OF MIAMI HISTORY. HE SCORED 31 TOUCHDOWNS IN JUST 21 GAMES!

McGAHEE BY THE NUMBERS
2004 SEASON ▶ RUSHING YARDS: 1,128 • YARDS PER CARRY: 4.0 • TOUCHDOWNS: 13
RECEPTIONS: 22 • RECEIVING YARDS: 169

Carson
PALMER

"I still have a **long way to go.**"

QUARTERBACK
CINCINNATI BENGALS

BORN: 12/27/79
HEIGHT: 6-5
WEIGHT: 230
COLLEGE: USC

NEVER SATISFIED

Carson Palmer's rookie year was a long one. The first player chosen in the 2003 NFL Draft, Carson arrived in Cincinnati with a mountain of hardware. The biggest award on his mantel: the Heisman Trophy, presented annually to the best player in college football. No wonder Bengals fans were excited. Like Carson, they would have to be patient: he spent his first season on the bench, watching, learning, and studying. When 2004 rolled around, he was handed the football. And Carson was ready! He started every game until hurting his knee late in the season. Along the way, he threw 18 touchdown passes and looked like one of the best young quarterbacks in the NFL. "Carson did a good job," observed Cincinnati offensive coordinator Bob Bratkowski, "but he hasn't really arrived yet. He's not as good as he's going to be." That's great news for the Bengals, and a warning for the rest of the league.

DID YOU KNOW? CARSON IS ONLY THE SECOND HEISMAN TROPHY WINNER DRAFTED BY THE BENGALS. THE FIRST WAS RUNNING BACK ARCHIE GRIFFIN, WHO WON THE AWARD IN BOTH 1974 AND 1975.

PALMER BY THE NUMBERS
2004 SEASON
COMPLETIONS: 263 • ATTEMPTS: 432 • PASSING YARDS: 2,897
TOUCHDOWNS: 18 • RATING: 77.3

Julius
PEPPERS

" I think I can be one of the **great ones."**

DEFENSIVE END
CAROLINA PANTHERS

BORN: 1/18/80
HEIGHT: 6-6
WEIGHT: 283
COLLEGE: NORTH CAROLINA

UNSTOPPABLE

You don't really stop Julius Peppers. You just try to slow him down a bit. One of the NFL's most athletic players, Julius presents a unique problem to opponents. First of all, he's huge. But that's only the beginning. Despite his size and strength, Julius is startlingly quick and agile. If you try to push him off the line of scrimmage, he'll just take a step back, give you a little fake, and go around you. Before you know it he's in the backfield, wreaking havoc. Julius isn't just a master of the quarterback sack. He can do it all: force fumbles, chase down running backs, intercept passes. He can even score touchdowns. Julius is such a gifted athlete that he could probably play professional basketball, as well as football. In fact, he played both sports at the University of North Carolina. But football is Julius' first love. Watching him play, it isn't hard to see why. He's awesome!

DID YOU KNOW? A KEY MEMBER OF THE NORTH CAROLINA TAR HEELS BASKETBALL TEAM, JULIUS IS THE ONLY PERSON TO PLAY IN BOTH THE SUPER BOWL AND THE FINAL FOUR OF THE NCAA TOURNAMENT.

PEPPERS BY THE NUMBERS
2004 SEASON

TOTAL TACKLES: 64 • SOLO TACKLES: 52 • ASSISTS: 12 • SACKS: 11
FORCED FUMBLES: 4 • INTERCEPTIONS: 2

Ed
REED

"I love football.
To know that I can **make a play,**
or maybe even **win** the game,
that's **exciting** to me. **"**

**SAFETY
BALTIMORE RAVENS**

BORN: 9/11/78
HEIGHT: 5-11
WEIGHT: 200
COLLEGE: MIAMI

RECORD BREAKER

When you play alongside Ray Lewis, one of the NFL's all-time great linebackers, it's easy to be overshadowed. But in 2004, Ed Reed stepped into the spotlight. An electrifying athlete with a nose for the ball, Ed became the first safety in twenty years to be named NFL Defensive Player of the Year. By dominating games from the secondary, Ed practically redesigned the blueprint for his position. He's smart, explosive, and fearless. He also knows how to make big plays. Not only did he lead the league in interceptions, but he set a record for return yards. You see, Ed doesn't believe the play is over when he intercepts a pass. It's just beginning. In his most memorable moment of the season, Ed picked off a pass in the end zone against the Cleveland Browns and returned it 106 yards for a touchdown! It was the longest return in NFL history, and another spot in the record books for Ed Reed.

DID YOU KNOW? ED HAS A KNACK FOR COMMUNICATION. HE TOOK GRADUATE-LEVEL CREATIVE WRITING COURSES WHILE HE WAS A STUDENT AT THE UNIVERSITY OF MIAMI. AND HAS BEEN A CORRESPONDENT FOR THE NFL NETWORK.

REED BY THE NUMBERS
2004 SEASON

TOTAL TACKLES: 76 • SOLO TACKLES: 62 • ASSISTS: 14 • SACKS: 2
INTERCEPTIONS: 9 • RETURN YARDS: 358 • TOUCHDOWNS: 2

Ben
ROETHLISBERGER

"I hate to lose."

QUARTERBACK
PITTSBURGH STEELERS

BORN: 3/2/82
HEIGHT: 6-4
WEIGHT: 241
COLLEGE: MIAMI (OH)

BIG BEN

NFL quarterbacks are made, not born. It's a demanding job that requires enormous skill, poise, and experience. That's why you hardly ever see a rookie QB break into the starting lineup. There's simply too much to learn. A rookie is supposed to watch . . . and wait. Unless, of course, the rookie's name is Ben Roethlisberger. With the size of a linebacker, the agility of a running back, and a cannon for an arm, Big Ben is hardly a typical quarterback. Combine those physical attributes with the poise of a natural leader, and you have a young man who promises to be a superstar for many years to come. That's good news for the Steelers, who didn't lose a single regular-season game in 2004 with Ben in the lineup. In fact, Ben is the first quarterback in NFL history to go undefeated in his first year. Not surprisingly, he was named NFL Offensive Rookie of the Year. So forget about waiting. Ben Roethlisberger's time is now.

DID YOU KNOW?

BEN WAS A LATE BLOOMER. TALL AND VERY SKINNY, HE HAD TO WAIT UNTIL HIS SENIOR YEAR IN HIGH SCHOOL TO START AT QUARTERBACK.

ROETHLISBERGER BY THE NUMBERS
2004 SEASON

COMPLETIONS: 196 • ATTEMPTS: 295 • PASSING YARDS: 2,621
TOUCHDOWNS: 17 • RATING: 98.1

Jonathan VILMA

" All I needed was an **opportunity.**"

**LINEBACKER
NEW YORK JETS**

BORN: 4/16/82
HEIGHT: 6-1
WEIGHT: 230
COLLEGE: MIAMI

ROOKIE OF THE YEAR

The New York Jets knew they had found a special player when they first saw Jonathan Vilma play at the University of Miami. It was obvious that someday he would make an impact in the NFL. But no one could have guessed that it would happen so quickly. Jonathan arrived at training camp in the summer of 2004 as just another rookie hoping to get a chance to play. He didn't make the Jets' starting lineup until the third game of the season. But after that, there was no turning back! An intense, aggressive player, Jonathan immediately made his presence felt. Despite his youth, he became the Jets' leader, calling signals on defense. He was second on the team in tackles, and his energy helped lift the Jets into the play-offs. Jonathan's performance was so impressive that he was named NFL Defensive Rookie of the Year. The only question now: What does he do for an encore?

DID YOU KNOW?

JONATHAN WAS A SERIOUS STUDENT IN COLLEGE WHO WAS NAMED TO THE BIG EAST ACADEMIC ALL-CONFERENCE TEAM THREE TIMES.

**VILMA BY THE NUMBERS
2004 SEASON**

TOTAL TACKLES: 107 • ASSISTS: 30 • SACKS: 2 • INTERCEPTIONS: 3
RETURN YARDS: 58 • TOUCHDOWNS 1

Brian
WESTBROOK

> "I do **different things** than other **running backs.**"

**RUNNING BACK
PHILADELPHIA EAGLES**

BORN: 9/2/79
HEIGHT: 5-10
WEIGHT: 205
COLLEGE: VILLANOVA

MULTIPLE THREAT

Opposing coaches lose a lot of sleep trying to figure out how to stop Brian Westbrook, a compact, explosive player who can break a game open any time he gets his hands on the ball. Brian is like a Ferrari: he goes from zero to sixty in a hurry. That means he can slip through the narrowest of openings. He takes the ball from the quarterback and — *Whoosh!* — he's gone! But that's only one of the weapons in Brian's arsenal. You see, he's also one of the NFL's top receivers. In leading the Eagles to the Super Bowl in 2004, he had more receptions and receiving yards than any other running back in the league. It's that versatility that makes Brian so unique — and so dangerous. When the ball is snapped, you never know what he's going to do: take the handoff, throw a crushing block for a teammate, or circle out of the backfield and catch a pass. Only one thing is certain: wherever the action is, that's where you'll find Brian Westbrook.

DID YOU KNOW?

BRIAN HOLDS THE NCAA DIVISION I-AA RECORD FOR TOTAL ALL-PURPOSE YARDS.

**WESTBROOK BY THE NUMBERS
2004 SEASON**
RUSHING YARDS: 812 • YARDS PER CARRY: 4.6 • TOUCHDOWNS: 3 • RECEPTIONS: 73
RECEIVING YARDS: 703 • YARDS PER CATCH: 9.6 • TOUCHDOWNS 6

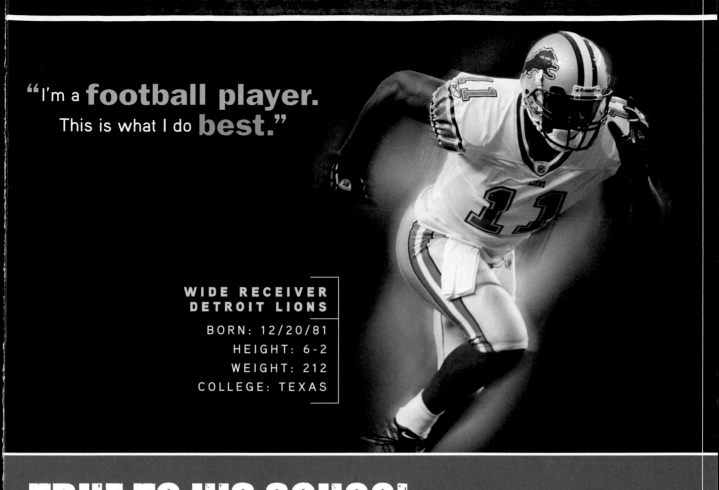

"I'm a **football player.**
This is what I do **best.**"

**WIDE RECEIVER
DETROIT LIONS**

BORN: 12/20/81
HEIGHT: 6-2
WEIGHT: 212
COLLEGE: TEXAS

TRUE TO HIS SCHOOL

Every professional athlete wants to make a name for himself. That can be difficult when you're a rookie in the NFL, and you share the name of an All-Pro safety. Such was the challenge faced by Roy Williams in 2004. Everyone knew about the other Roy Williams, a superstar defender with the Dallas Cowboys. But what about this guy, the wide receiver from the University of Texas? Well, the confusion has ended. With spectacular speed and leaping ability, and an uncanny ability to hang on to the ball, the new Roy Williams has emerged as a star in his own right. Not only did he lead the Lions in receiving, he set a Lions rookie record for receptions with 54. In other words, he didn't play like a rookie. Roy is already being compared favorably to some of the greatest receivers who have played, such as Jerry Rice and Terrell Owens. But make no mistake: while there may be two guys named Roy Williams in the NFL, this wide receiver is a singular talent.

DID YOU KNOW?
ROY HAD A SMALL ROLE IN THE HIT MOVIE *FRIDAY NIGHT LIGHTS*, WHICH WAS FILMED IN HIS HOMETOWN OF ODESSA, TEXAS.

WILLIAMS BY THE NUMBERS
2004 SEASON ▶ RECEPTIONS: 54 • RECEIVING YARDS: 817 • YARDS PER CATCH: 15.1
LONGEST RECEPTION: 46 • TOUCHDOWNS: 8

NFL LEADERS

RUSHING YARDS

2004	Curtis Martin	1,697
2003	Jamal Lewis	2,066
2002	Ricky Williams	1,853
2001	Priest Holmes	1,555
2000	Edgerrin James	1,709
1999	Edgerrin James	1,553
1998	Terrell Davis	2,008
1997	Barry Sanders	2,053
1996	Barry Sanders	1,553
1995	Emmitt Smith	1,773
1994	Barry Sanders	1,883
1993	Emmitt Smith	1,486
1992	Emmitt Smith	1,713
1991	Emmitt Smith	1,563
1990	Barry Sanders	1,304

PASSING YARDS

2004	Daunte Cilpepper	4,717
2003	Peyton Manning	4,267
2002	Rich Gannon	4,689
2001	Kurt Warner	4,830
2000	Peyton Manning	4,413
1999	Steve Beuerlein	4,436
1998	Brett Favre	4,212
1997	Jeff George	3,917
1996	Mark Brunell	4,367
1995	Brett Favre	4,413
1994	Drew Bledsoe	4,555
1993	John Elway	4,030
1992	Dan Marino	4,116
1991	Warren Moon	4,690
1990	Warren Moon	4,689

PASS RECEIVING YARDS

2004	Muhsin Muhammad	1,405
2003	Torry Holt	1,696
2002	Marvin Harrison	1,722
2001	David Boston	1,598
2000	Torry Holt	1,635
1999	Marvin Harrison	1,663
1998	Antonio Freeman	1,424
1997	Rob Moore	1,584
1996	Isaac Bruce	1,338
1995	Jerry Rice	1,848
1994	Jerry Rice	1,499
1993	Jerry Rice	1,503
1992	Sterling Sharpe	1,461
1991	Michael Irvin	1,523
1990	Jerry Rice	1,502

SACKS

2004	Dwight Freeney	16.0
2003	Michael Strahan	18.5
2002	Jason Taylor	18.5
2001	Michael Strahan	22.5
2000	La'Roi Glover	17.0
1999	Kevin Carter	17.0
1998	Michael Sinclair	16.5
1997	John Randle	15.5
1996	Kevin Greene	14.5
1995	Bryce Paup	17.5
1994	Kevin Greene	14.0
1993	Neil Smith	15.0
1992	Clyde Simmons	19.0
1991	Pat Swilling	17.0
1990	Derrick Thomas	20.0